GREAT KEYBOARD SONATAS

Carl Philipp Emanuel
BACH

Series II

Dover Publications, Inc.
NEW YORK

Published in Canada by General Publishing Company, Ltd., 30 Lesmill Road, Don Mills, Toronto, Ontario.

Published in the United Kingdom by Constable and Company, Ltd., 10 Orange Street, London WC2H 7EG.

This Dover edition, first published in 1985, is a new selection, arranged in a new sequence, of sonatas by C. P. E. Bach as published within Volumes XII and XIII of *Le Trésor des Pianistes*, edited by Aristide and Louise Farrenc, Paris, 1861–1874. Series I of the Dover edition contains sonatas composed between 1731 and 1751; Series II, sonatas composed between 1752 and 1784. See the table of contents for original publication years of the various sonatas, original composition years and Wotquenne numbers.

Manufactured in the United States of America
Dover Publications, Inc., 31 East 2nd Street, Mineola, N.Y. 11501

Library of Congress Cataloging in Publication Data

Bach, Carl Philipp Emanuel, 1714–1788.
   [Sonatas, keyboard instrument. Selections]
   Great keyboard sonatas.

   (v. of music)
   Originally published in v. 12–13 of Le trésor des pianistes, edited by Aristide and Louise Farrenc, Paris, 1861–1874.
   1. Sonatas (Harpsichord)   2. Sonatas (Clavichord)   3. Sonatas (Piano)   I. Title.
M23.B12F4   1985   84-759591
ISBN 0-486-24853-4 (v. 1)
ISBN 0-486-24854-2 (v. 2)

CONTENTS

The present volume contains sonatas composed between 1752 and 1784. The sequence is by year of composition, except that the sonatas from the *Kenner und Liebhaber* volumes are all placed together at the end in the order of their publication in those volumes. Only those years of first publication are given that fall within the composer's lifetime or the first generation after his death. The W numbers are those assigned to the sonatas in the standard work by Alfred Wotquenne, *Thematisches Verzeichnis der Werke von Carl Philipp Emanuel Bach (1714–1788)*, Leipzig, 1905.

GREAT
KEYBOARD
SONATAS

Sonata in G Minor, W.65/27

Larghetto.

Allegro.

Sonata in E-flat Major, W.65/28

Andante.

Sonata in D Minor, W.62/15

Larghetto.

Sonata in C Minor, W.65/31

Allegro assai ma pomposo.

Allegro.

Sonata in E Major, W.62/17

Sonata in E Major, W.62/17

ALLEGRETTO.

Sonata in B-flat Major, W.62/16

ANDANTE.

ALLEGRETTO.

Sonata in G Minor, W.62/18

Sonata in G Major, W.62/19

Presto.

Sonata in B Minor, W.62/22

Adagio.

Allegretto.

Sonata in A Minor, W.62/21

ADAGIO.

ALLEGRETTO SICILIANO E SCHERZANDO.

Sonata in A Major, W.65/37

Andante
ma non
troppo.

Allegro
molto.

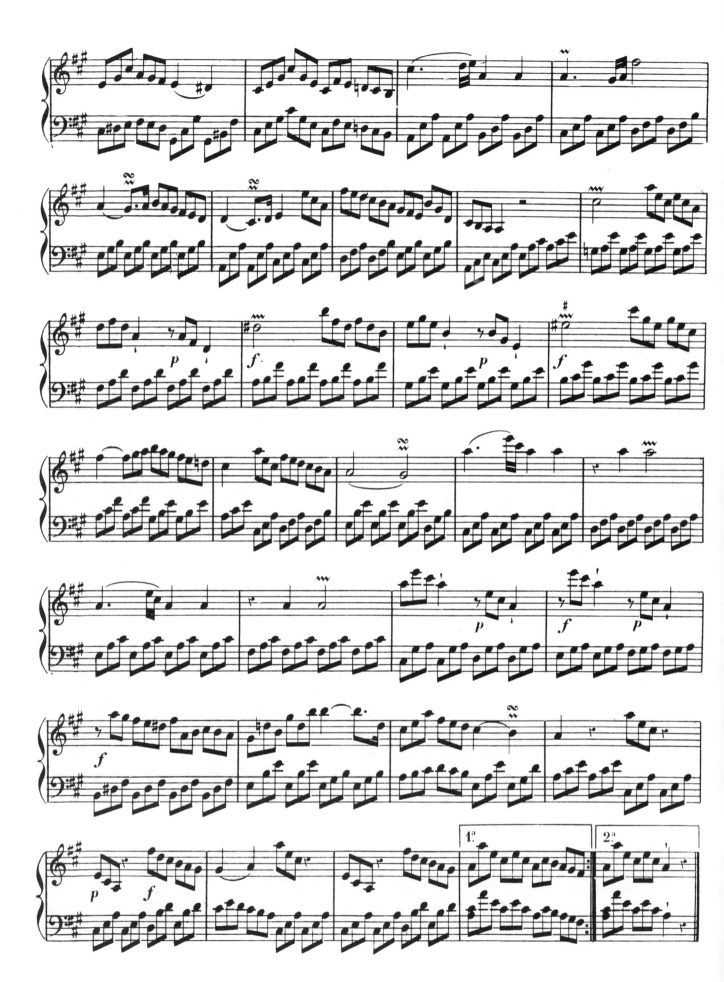

Sonata in E Minor, W.65/39

Largo con tenerezza.

Sonata in D Major, W.65/40

Larghetto

FINE.

Sonata in G Minor, W.65/44

Allegro assai.

Sonata in E Major, W.65/46

Larghetto.

Sonata in C Major, W.55/1 (*Kenner und Liebhaber* I,1)

110   Sonata in C Major, W.55/1 (*Kenner und Liebhaber* I,1)

Andante.

Sonata in C Major, W.55/1 (*Kenner und Liebhaber* I,1)

Sonata in F Major, W.55/2 (*Kenner und Liebhaber* I,2)

Larghetto.

Sonata in A Major, W.55/4 *(Kenner und Liebhaber I,4)*

Allegro assai.

124   Sonata in A Major, W.55/4 (*Kenner und Liebhaber* I,4)

Sonata in A Major, W.55/4 (*Kenner und Liebhaber* I,4)

Poco Adagio.

Sonata in G Major, W.55/6 (*Kenner und Liebhaber* I,6)

Andante.

Sonata in G Major, W.56/2 (*Kenner und Liebhaber* II,2)

Larghetto.

Allegro.

Sonata in F Major, W.56/4 (*Kenner und Liebhaber* II,4)

V. S.

Sonata in A Minor, W.57/2 (*Kenner und Liebhaber* III,2)

Andante.

Allegro di molto.

Sonata in D Minor, W.57/4 (*Kenner und Liebhaber* III,4)

Cantabile
e mesto.

Sonata in D Minor, W.57/4 (*Kenner und Liebhaber* III,4)

Sonata in F Minor, W.57/6 (*Kenner und Liebhaber* III,6)

Andante.

Rondo.

Sonata in B-flat Major, W.59/3 *(Kenner und Liebhaber* V,3)

Largo.

Andantino grazioso.